christmas at home

101 FAVORITE HOLIDAY

Recipes

Ellyn Sanna

BARBOUR

PUBLISHING, INC.
Uhrichsville, Ohio
Printed in Canada

Published by Barbour Publishing, Inc., P.O. Box 719, Uhrichsville, Ohio 44683
http://www.barbourbooks.com

 Member of the
Evangelical Christian
Publishers Association

Printed in Canada.

contents

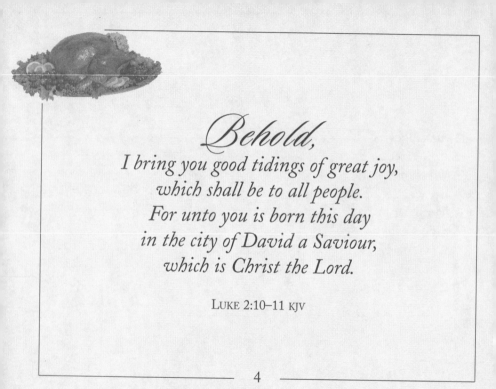

Behold,
I bring you good tidings of great joy,
which shall be to all people.
For unto you is born this day
in the city of David a Saviour,
which is Christ the Lord.

LUKE 2:10–11 KJV

At Christmas, we celebrate the birthday of Jesus, the Son of God. His birth into our world changed the lives of all of us forever, for His life brings love and freedom and eternal joy. What better way to honor the birth of God's Son than by gathering with those we love for times of feasting and togetherness! As Paul said in his first letter to the Corinthians, "Therefore let us keep the feast." And as we celebrate with food and holiday gatherings, let us always remember to keep Christ at the center of each Christmas meal.

If anyone hears my voice and opens the door,
I will come in and eat with him, and he with me.

REVELATION 3:20 NIV

You prepare a feast for me. . .
My cup overflows with blessings.

PSALM 23:5 NLT

6

1

BEVERAGES

Love and joy come to you,
And to you your wassail too,
And God bless you and send you a happy new year.

OLD ENGLISH CAROL

Hot Cran-Apple Cider

2 quarts apple cider
1½ quarts cranberry juice cocktail
¼ cup packed brown sugar, if desired
4 three-inch sticks cinnamon
1½ tsp whole cloves
1 lemon, thinly sliced

Mix all ingredients together in a large kettle and bring to a boil.
Reduce heat and simmer uncovered until flavors are blended, about
15 minutes. Remove cinnamon, cloves, and lemon slices. Serve fresh
lemon slices in each cup if desired.

Frosty Lime Punch

2 cans (6 ounces each) frozen limeade concentrate, thawed
3 cups cold water
2 bottles (12 ounces each) lemon-lime carbonated beverage,
   chilled
1 cup lime sherbet

In a large punch bowl, mix limeade concentrate, cold water and carbonated beverage. Spoon scoops of sherbet into bowl and serve immediately. Makes about 15 ½-cup servings.

Christmas Punch

1 quart bottle grape juice
1 pint of lemon juice
½ pint of pineapple juice,
   or other sweet juice

1 pint of orange juice
1 bottle of carbonated water
1 pint of ginger ale

Mix all ingredients and pour into a punch bowl with a block of ice. Sliced pineapples or oranges may be used as a garnish. Makes about 2 gallons of punch.

Wassail

1 gallon apple cider
2 tsp whole allspice
2 tsp whole cloves

2 three-inch sticks cinnamon
$2/3$ cup sugar
orange slices, studded with
cloves

Combine all but orange slices in a kettle and bring to a boil.
Reduce heat, cover, and simmer 20 minutes. Strain punch and
pour into a heat-resistant punch bowl. Float orange slices in bowl.
Makes about 32 $1/2$-cup servings.

Mexican Atole or Champurrado

*A cornmeal brew drunk in Mexico
during the Christmas season.*

½ cup masa flour (Mexican corn flour used for tamale dough and
available packaged in Mexican neighborhoods and some
supermarkets)

2 cups water

1 stick cinnamon

4 cups milk

2 cups brown sugar

3 ounces unsweetened
chocolate

Stir together masa and water; add cinnamon and cook over low
heat, stirring frequently until thick. Blend in milk, sugar and chocolate, beating with a wire whisk until smooth. Cook slowly and
bring to a boil once more and serve. Makes about 6 servings.

Citrus Fizz

Very simple—yet refreshing!

6 cups fresh orange or grapefruit juice, chilled
2 cups club soda

Mix juice and soda in a glass pitcher. Stir briefly and serve immediately.

sparkling cranberry punch

2 quarts cranberry juice cocktail, chilled
1 can (6 ounces) frozen lemonade concentrate, thawed
1 quart sparkling water

Mix cranberry juice cocktail and lemonade concentrate in a large punch bowl. Just before serving, stir in chilled sparkling water. Makes 25 ½-cup servings.

Orchard Fizz

10 sugar cubes
2 lemons, thinly sliced
¾ cup lime juice
4⅓ cups sparkling apple juice
1 cup soda water (club soda)

2 limes, thinly sliced
2 kiwi fruits, peeled and
    thinly sliced
mint sprigs

Rub sugar cubes over lemons to remove zest, and place a cube in each glass. After squeezing, combine juice from lemons with lime juice, apple juice, and soda water. Float fruit slices and mint sprigs on top and serve in chilled glasses.

Eggnog

4 eggs, separated
½ cup sugar
2 cups cold milk
1 cup cold light cream

1½ tsp. vanilla
⅛ tsp salt
¼ tsp nutmeg

Beat eggs together with ¼ cup sugar until thick. Gradually mix in milk, cream, vanilla, salt, and nutmeg, beating until frothy. Beat egg whites with remaining sugar until mixture forms soft peaks; then fold into egg yolk mixture. Cover and chill. Mix well before serving and sprinkle with nutmeg.

2

APPETIZERS

At Christmas play, and make good cheer,
For Christmas comes but once a year.

THOMAS TUSSER

Parmesan Bread Sticks

1 loaf (1 lb.) French bread
¾ cup margarine or butter, melted
¼ cup grated Parmesan cheese

Preheat oven to 425°. Cut bread loaf into 5 pieces, each about 4 inches long. Cut each piece lengthwise into 6 sticks. After brushing sides with melted margarine and sprinkling with Parmesan cheese, place sticks on ungreased jelly roll pan and bake about 8 minutes, or until golden. Makes about 30 bread sticks.

Cherry Tomato Blossoms

1 pint medium to large cherry tomatoes (about 24)
2 ounces cream cheese, cut into ½-inch cubes (about 24)

Placing tomatoes stem side down, cut each into fourths (*almost* through to bottom). Insert cheese cube in center of each tomato. Top with small parsley springs to garnish. Makes about 2 dozen appetizers.

Mushrooms stuffed with crab

24 medium mushrooms
   (about 1 pound)
3 tbsp butter or olive oil
1 shallot, minced
1 package (8-ounce)
   cream cheese, softened
1 can (6-ounce) crabmeat

1 tbsp lemon juice
1 tbsp minced parsley
½ tsp prepared
   white horseradish
¼ tsp salt
dash of cayenne

Remove and finely chop stems of mushrooms. Melt 1 tbsp butter in skillet over medium heat. Add shallot and mushroom stems and cook about 3 minutes, or until mushroom liquid has evaporated. Pour mixture into a medium bowl and add cream cheese, crabmeat, lemon juice, parsley, horseradish, salt, and cayenne, blending well. Melt remaining butter in skillet over medium heat. Remove from heat and toss mushroom caps in skillet until well coated with butter. Place caps stem end up on a baking sheet and fill with 2 tsp crab mixture. Bake 10 minutes, or until filling is bubbly and mushrooms are tender.

Salmon Party Ball

1 package (8 ounces)
   cream cheese, softened
1 can (16 ounces) salmon,
   drained and flaked
1 tbsp finely chopped onion

1 tbsp lemon juice
1/4 tsp liquid smoke
1/4 tsp salt
1/3 cup chopped nuts
1/4 cup snipped parsley

Mixing all ingredients except nuts and parsley, shape mixture into a ball. Cover and chill at least 8 hours. Coat ball with parsley and nut mixture.

Hot Sausage and Cheese Puffs

1 pound hot or sweet Italian sausage
1 pound sharp cheddar cheese, shredded
3 cups biscuit baking mix
$3/4$ cup water

Cook sausage, breaking up with fork until no longer pink. Drain and cool completely. Combine cheese, sausage, baking mix, and water. Mix with fork until just blended. Roll into 1-inch balls and place on baking sheet. Bake at 400° for 12 to 15 minutes. Makes about 100 puffs.

cucumbers stuffed with feta cheese

2 medium English (hothouse) cucumbers, scrubbed
1 package (8-ounce) cream cheese, softened
½ cup crumbled feta cheese
2 tbsp chopped fresh dill or 2 tsp dried dill

Remove cucumber ends and cut in half lengthwise. Remove seeds from both halves with a melon baller and set aside. Blend cream cheese, feta cheese and dill until well mixed. Spoon cheese mixture into each cucumber half and reassemble halves, pressing together gently. Wrap in plastic wrap and chill. Before serving, cut into ½-inch slices.

Bacon Crispies

6 ounces finely chopped bacon
¾ cup butter, softened
1½ cups all-purpose flour

salt and pepper
½ cup grated cheddar
  cheese

Heat oven to 325°. Beat butter, flour, salt and pepper until smooth. Add grated cheese and ⅔ bacon and mix well. Drop by teaspoonfuls onto greased baking sheet, sprinkling with remaining bacon. Bake for 30 minutes or until lightly browned. Cool and store in airtight tin. Makes 28–30 appetizers.

Quick Brie en croute

1 small garlic clove, crushed through a press
2 tbsp extra-virgin olive oil
1 round loaf (1 to 1½ pound) French or Italian bread
1 wheel (8 ounce) of Brie
1 tbsp minced parsley

Preheat oven to 350°. Stir garlic in olive oil and set aside. Slice and remove top third of bread loaf. Place cheese wheel on center of bread, tracing around and cutting down as deep as cheese is high (about 1 to 1½ inches), and remove center for cheese. Cut ½-inch slices around edges of bread, but do not cut through bottom of loaf. Brush garlic oil over cut surfaces of bread and sprinkle with parsley. Leaving rind, score top of cheese several times and insert into center of loaf. Wrap loosely in foil and place on a baking sheet. Bake about 30 minutes or until bread is lightly toasted and cheese begins to melt. When cool enough, guests may serve themselves by pulling off slices and spreading the melted cheese with a small knife. Serves 6 to 8.

Miniature Ham Puffs

1 cup water
½ cup margarine or butter
1 cup all-purpose flour
3 cans (4½ ounces each)
    deviled ham

4 eggs
1 tbsp horseradish
¾ tsp pepper
¾ tsp onion salt
⅓ cup dairy sour cream

Heat oven to 400°. In saucepan, bring water and margarine to a rolling boil. Add flour and stir vigorously over low heat for about 1 minute, or until mixture forms a ball; remove from heat. Beat in eggs, all at once, until smooth and glossy. Drop dough by teaspoonfuls onto ungreased cookie sheet. Bake about 25 minutes, or until puffed, golden brown and dry. Cool on wire racks. Mix deviled ham, horseradish, pepper, onion salt and sour cream; chill. Just before serving, remove tops of puffs with sharp knife, scooping out any filaments of soft dough. Fill each puff with ham mixture. Makes 5 to 6 dozen appetizers.

Festive Nibbles

1 cup all-purpose flour, plus extra for dusting
1 tsp mustard powder
salt
½ cup butter, plus extra for greasing
3 ounces cheddar cheese, grated
pinch of cayenne
2 tbsp water
1 egg, beaten
poppy seeds, sunflower seeds,
    or sesame seeds, to decorate

Sift together flour, mustard powder, and salt. Cut butter into mixture until it resembles fine bread crumbs. Stir in the cheese and cayenne and sprinkle on the water. Add half the beaten egg, mix to a firm dough, and knead lightly until smooth. Roll out dough on a lightly floured board. Cut out desired shapes and place on a greased baking sheet, brushing tops with remaining egg. Sprinkle seeds over top to decorate and bake for 10 minutes.

chicken Bites

4 chicken breasts, boned and skinned
1 cup finely crushed round buttery crackers (about 24)
$\frac{1}{2}$ cup grated Parmesan cheese
$\frac{1}{4}$ cup finely chopped walnuts
1 tsp dried thyme leaves
1 tsp dried basil leaves
$\frac{1}{2}$ tsp seasoned salt
$\frac{1}{4}$ tsp pepper
$\frac{1}{2}$ cup margarine or butter, melted

Place aluminum foil over 2 baking sheets. Cut chicken into 1-inch pieces. Combine cracker crumbs, Parmesan cheese, walnuts, thyme, basil, seasoned salt, and pepper. Heat oven to 400°. Dip chicken pieces into melted margarine, then into crumb mixture. Place chicken pieces on cookie sheets and bake uncovered for 20–25 minutes, or until golden brown. Makes about 6 dozen appetizers.

3
VEGETABLES

Then let us all most merry be,
And sing with cheerful voice,
For we have good occasion now
This time for to rejoice.

OLD ENGLISH CAROL

Mixed Vegetable Medley

1 package (10 ounces) frozen peas
1 package (10 ounces) frozen green beans
1 package (10 ounces) frozen cauliflower
3/4 cup water
1 jar (2 ounces) sliced pimiento, drained
2 tbsp margarine or butter
1/2 tsp dried basil leaves
1/2 tsp salt
1/8 tsp pepper

Bring vegetables and water to a boil and reduce heat. Cover and cook over low heat about 7 minutes or until vegetables are tender. Drain and stir in remaining ingredients.

cinnamon sweet potatoes

2½ pounds sweet potatoes or
    yams (7 or 8 medium)
½ cup packed brown sugar
¼ cup margarine or butter

3 tbsp water
½ tsp ground
    cinnamon
½ tsp salt

Heat salted water (½ tsp salt to 1 cup water) to boiling. Add potatoes. Cover and bring back to a boil, cooking 30 to 35 minutes, or until tender. Drain. Remove skins. Cut potatoes crosswise into ½-inch slices. Combine brown sugar, margarine, water, cinnamon, and salt in 10-inch skillet. Cook over medium heat, stirring constantly until smooth. Add potato slices and stir until glazed and heated through.

Antipasto Toss

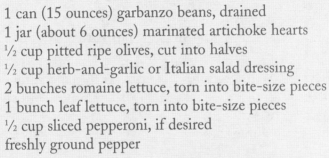

1 can (15 ounces) garbanzo beans, drained
1 jar (about 6 ounces) marinated artichoke hearts
$\frac{1}{2}$ cup pitted ripe olives, cut into halves
$\frac{1}{2}$ cup herb-and-garlic or Italian salad dressing
2 bunches romaine lettuce, torn into bite-size pieces
1 bunch leaf lettuce, torn into bite-size pieces
$\frac{1}{2}$ cup sliced pepperoni, if desired
freshly ground pepper

Mix beans, artichoke hearts (with liquid), olives, and salad dressing. Cover and refrigerate. Toss with remaining ingredients just before serving.

Green Peas with Celery and Onion

2 packages (10 ounces each)
  frozen peas
½ cup sliced celery
1 small onion, thinly sliced

3 tbsp margarine or
  butter, softened
¼ tsp salt

Following directions on package for peas, cook celery, onion, and peas; drain. Stir in margarine and salt.

Brussels sprouts and chestnuts

2¼ pounds Brussels sprouts
2 cups chicken stock
salt (optional)
2 tbsp butter

1 can (8-ounces) chestnuts,
  rinsed and drained
freshly ground black pepper

Cut a slice from base of each Brussels sprout and tear off outer leaves. Bring chicken stock to a boil in pan and place steamer containing sprouts over pan and cover. Steam for 6–8 minutes until sprouts are tender. Stir sprouts and chestnuts in melted butter over medium heat for 2–3 minutes. Transfer to a warm serving dish and season with pepper. Serves 8.

spinach-cucumber salad

8 ounces spinach, torn
    into bite-size pieces (about 8 cups)
2 medium cucumbers, thinly sliced
½ cup vegetable oil
2 tbsp sugar

2 tbsp vinegar
2 tsp soy sauce
½ tsp dry mustard
¼ tsp garlic powder

Put spinach and cucumbers in plastic bag; close tightly, and refrigerate for up to 24 hours. Mix remaining ingredients in a tightly covered jar and refrigerate. Prior to serving, shake dressing and toss with spinach and cucumbers.

Glazed carrots

1¼ pounds fresh carrots
(about 8 medium)
⅓ cup packed brown sugar

2 tbsp margarine or butter

½ tsp salt
½ tsp grated orange peel

Cut carrots in sections 2½ inch in length, then into ⅜ inch strips. Bring 1 inch salted water to a boil. Add carrots, cover, and bring to a boil again. Reduce heat and cook 18 to 20 minutes, or until tender; drain. Combine brown sugar, margarine, salt, and orange peel in a 10-inch skillet; stir and cook until bubbly. Add carrots and cook over low heat about 5 minutes, or until carrots are glazed and heated through.

Mixed Green Salad
with Parmesan Walnuts

1 small head lettuce
1 small bunch leaf lettuce
½ small bunch endive
4 ounces spinach

¼ cup oil and vinegar
 salad dressing
Parmesan Walnuts
 (next page)

Tear salad greens into bite-size pieces and toss with salad dressing until well-coated. Stir in ½ to 1 cup Parmesan Walnuts.

Parmesan Walnuts

1 tbsp margarine or butter
⅛ tsp hickory smoked salt
⅛ tsp salt

1 cup walnuts
2 tbsp grated
    Parmesan cheese

Place margarine, hickory salt, and salt, in a 9 x 9 x 2 inch baking pan and heat in a 350° oven 2 to 3 minutes, or until bubbly. Stir in walnuts and heat 5 minutes. Add Parmesan cheese and stir; return to oven for 3 to 5 minutes until cheese is lightly browned. Cool.

Asparagus with Pimiento

2 packages (10 ounces each)
   frozen asparagus spears
lemon juice

margarine or butter
pimiento strips

Cook frozen asparagus spears according to package directions and drain. Drizzle with lemon juice and melted butter or margarine. Garnish with pimiento strips.

Lemon-Glazed Beets

1/3 cup lemon or orange
    marmalade
1 tbsp vinegar

2 cans (16 ounces each)
    sliced beets

Combine lemon or orange marmalade and vinegar in 2-quart sauce-pan. Stir in drained, sliced beets; cover and heat about 10 minutes or until just heated through.

sweet potato crunch

3 pounds sweet potatoes
1 stick unsalted butter, melted
½ cup packed brown sugar
¼ cup orange juice

1½ tsp cinnamon
¼ tsp salt
1½ cups graham
     cracker crumbs

Place sweet potatoes in a pot of boiling water and cook for 35 to 40 minutes, or until tender; drain. When cool, peel. Preheat oven to 400°. Mash sweet potatoes in a large bowl; add 4 tbsp butter, brown sugar, orange juice, cinnamon, and salt; and mix until smooth. In a separate bowl, mix graham cracker crumbs and remaining 4 tbsp butter. Pour sweet potato mixture into a greased 9-inch square baking pan and top with butter and crumbs. Bake 15 to 20 minutes or until hot and bubbly. Serves 8 to 10.

Green Bean Buffet Salad

3 pounds fresh green beans
1 jar (7 ounces) roasted red peppers
½ medium sweet onion
    (yellow, white, or purple),
    sliced paper thin (optional)

Balsamic Vinaigrette
    (recipe on next page)
½ cup oil-cured black
    olives, pitted

Snap off bean ends, and if large, cut in half. Heat a kettle of salted water to boiling and add beans. When water returns to a rolling boil, cook 3 to 5 minutes, until crisp-tender. Drain in colander and rinse under cold running water. Drain liquid from roasted peppers and cut into ¼-inch strips. Toss lightly with green beans and onion slices. Prior to serving, pour vinaigrette over vegetables and toss until well coated. Scatter olives over top.

Balsamic Vinaigrette

1 garlic clove, crushed
1 tbsp Dijon mustard
¼ cup balsamic vinegar
¾ cup extra-virgin olive oil

¼ tsp salt
½ tsp pepper
1 tbsp chopped
   parsley

Place all but parsley in blender and blend for 2 minutes. Stir in parsley. If not used immediately, may be refrigerated up to 3 days.

caramelized carrots and pearl onions

1½ pounds carrots, peeled
   and cut into thin rings
8 ounces pearl onions, peeled
salt
3 tbsp butter

6 tbsp chicken stock
1 tbsp sugar
freshly ground
      black pepper

Bring carrots and onions to a boil in a pan of salted water over high heat. Boil for 1 minute and drain. Return to pan, add butter, chicken stock, and sugar and bring to a boil over medium heat, stirring occasionally. Cover and simmer over low heat until all liquid has been absorbed into vegetables and they are glossy and dry. Season with salt and pepper, and serve.

Golden Squash Casserole

6 cups cubed pared
  Hubbard squash*
1 cup dairy sour cream
2 tbsp margarine or butter

1 medium onion,
  finely chopped
1 tsp salt
¼ tsp pepper

Place 1 inch of salted water in pan and bring to a boil. Add squash, cover, and return to a boil. Cook 15 to 20 minutes or until tender; drain. After mashing squash, stir in remaining ingredients. Pour into ungreased, 1-quart casserole. Bake uncovered in a 325° oven for 35 to 45 minutes or until hot.

*2 packages (12 ounces each) frozen cooked squash, thawed, can be substituted for the cooked fresh squash.

Cheddar Corn Casserole with Red and Green Peppers

1 stick (4 ounces) butter, melted
1 large onion, chopped
½ medium green bell pepper, diced
½ medium red bell pepper, diced
1 garlic clove, minced
3 eggs

1 cup sour cream
1 can (16 ounces) cream-style corn
⅓ cup yellow cornmeal
¼ tsp salt
¼ tsp pepper
1¼ cups (5 ounces) shredded cheddar cheese

Preheat oven to 350°. Melt butter in a medium-sized skillet over medium heat. Add onion and green and red peppers, and cook, stirring occasionally for 3 to 5 minutes or until soft. Add garlic and cook an additional 1 to 2 minutes; remove from heat and set aside. Combine remaining butter, eggs, and sour cream in a large bowl and whisk until smooth. Stir in corn, cornmeal, salt, and pepper. Add cheese and cooked onion, peppers, and garlic. Pour into greased 2-quart casserole and bake for 30 to 35 minutes until puffed, golden, and set in center. Serves 8 to 10.

carrots in gravy

3 tbsp butter
2 pounds carrots, peeled
    and cut ½ inch thick
1 medium onion, chopped
2 tbsp flour

1 tbsp minced parsley
1 cup unsalted chicken stock
½ tsp salt
¼ tsp pepper
¼ tsp grated nutmeg

Melt butter in a large, heavy saucepan over low heat. Add carrots, cover, and cook, stirring occasionally for 20 to 25 minutes, until firm-tender. Place carrots in a bowl with slotted spoon. Add onion to butter remaining in saucepan. Increase heat to medium and cook until lightly browned. Sprinkle in flour and cook, stirring constantly until flour is golden. Add parsley and whisk in stock. Bring to a boil, continuing to whisk until gravy is smooth and thick. Season with salt, pepper, and nutmeg. Return carrots to saucepan and reduce heat to low, cooking until heated through. Serve hot.

4

BREADS

So, now is come our joyful feast,
Let every soul be jolly!

GEORGE WITHER

Cranberry-Orange Nut Bread

2 cups all-purpose flour
¾ cup sugar
1½ tsp baking powder
¾ tsp salt
½ tsp baking soda
¼ cup margarine or butter, softened

1 tbsp grated orange peel
¾ cup orange juice
1 egg
1 cup cranberries, chopped
½ cup chopped nuts

Heat oven to 350°. Grease bottom only of 9 x 5 x 3 loaf pan. Combine flour, sugar, baking powder, salt, and baking soda; cut in margarine until crumbly. Add orange peel, orange juice, and egg, and stir just until moistened. Mix in cranberries and nuts. Pour into prepared pan and bake 55 to 65 minutes, or until wooden toothpick inserted in center comes out clean. Cool completely before slicing.

Potato Rosemary Bread

2 medium baking potatoes,
  peeled and cut into
  1-inch chunks
½ tsp minced rosemary
2 cups flour

1 envelope (½ ounce)
  active dry yeast
½ tsp salt
½ tsp pepper

Cook potatoes in boiling water for 15 minutes or until tender. Drain, reserving 1¼ cups of potato water. Pour into a large bowl adding rosemary, and allowing to cool until tepid. Add yeast and leave 5 to 10 minutes to dissolve. Add flour, salt, and pepper to yeast mixture and stir to make a firm dough. Knead on lightly floured board for 15 to 20 minutes or until dough is smooth. Work mashed potatoes into dough. Place dough in a large, clean bowl, cover with kitchen towel and allow to rise 1 hour or until doubled in size. Punch down and shape into round loaf and place on greased baking sheet. Allow to rise again until doubled in size, about 30 minutes. (Preheat oven to 350° about 15 minutes before end of rising time.) Bake 45 to 50 minutes or until top of loaf is brown and bottom sounds hollow when tapped.

Irish Soda Bread

4 cups flour
1 cup dark raisins
1 cup golden raisins
¼ cup sugar
1 tsp baking soda

1 tsp salt
2 cups buttermilk
1 egg
Honey Butter
  (recipe follows)

Preheat oven to 350° and grease 9-inch round cake pan. Stir together flour, dark raisins, golden raisins, sugar, baking soda, and salt in a large bowl until well mixed. Make a well in the center. In another bowl, combine buttermilk and egg. Beat until well blended and pour into well of flour mixture. Using your hands, mix thoroughly. Mound dough into prepared pan and smooth top with hands. To ensure even baking, score a cross on top of loaf. Bake until a golden crust forms and loaf sounds hollow when tapped, about 1 hour. Cool and serve warm or at room temperature with Honey Butter.

HONEY BUTTER

2 sticks (8 ounces) butter,   ½ to ⅔ cup honey,
   softened   to taste

Blend butter and honey in a food processor or blender. Chill until barely firm and shape into 2 to 4 cylinders. Seal in plastic wrap. May be refrigerated for up to 10 days.

Cinnamon, Raisin, and Walnut Batter Bread

1 envelope (1/4 ounce) active
  dry yeast
1½ cups warm water
  (105° to 115°)
2 tbsp honey
2 cups whole wheat flour
1 cup all-purpose flour

1 tsp cinnamon
1 tsp salt
2 tbsp butter, softened
1 cup raisins
½ cup chopped toasted
  walnuts

Place water in large bowl and dissolve yeast. Whisk in honey. Add whole wheat flour, all-purpose flour, cinnamon, and salt, and mix until well blended. Stir in raisins, walnuts, and butter, and mix well. Place dough in bowl to rise and cover with a kitchen towel. Leave until doubled in size, about 40 to 50 minutes. With a spoon, stir dough down and transfer to well greased 9 x 5 x 3 inch loaf pan. Cover and allow to rise in a warm place for about 20 to 30 minutes, or until dough has reached top of pan. Preheat oven to 400° about 15 minutes before end of rising time. Bake for 30 to 35 minutes, or until loaf bottom sounds hollow when tapped and top of bread is golden. Remove from pan immediately and cool on rack.

Gingerbread Muffins

1 tsp baking soda
½ cup buttermilk
¾ cup solid vegetable
   shortening
½ cup granulated sugar
½ cup packed dark
   brown sugar

2 eggs
½ cup dark corn syrup
2 cups flour
2 tsp ground ginger
1½ tsp cinnamon
½ tsp ground allspice
½ tsp ground cloves

Pour buttermilk in a small bowl; add baking soda, and dissolve, stirring to blend. In a separate bowl at medium speed, beat shortening, granulated sugar, and brown sugar for about 5 minutes, or until light and fluffy. Add eggs one at a time while continuing to blend with electric mixer. Blend in corn syrup. Sift together flour, ginger, cinnamon, allspice, and cloves in a medium bowl. Add to butter mixture, alternating with buttermilk mixture, being sure to beat well after each addition. Cover and refrigerate for 24 hours. Preheat oven to 350°. Grease muffin tins and spoon in batter, filling cups about three-fourths full. Bake 20 to 25 minutes, or until only moist crumbs cling to knife inserted into muffins. Yields 24 muffins.

Holiday Streusel Coffee Cake

Streusel (next page)
2 cups all-purpose flour
1 cup sugar
3 tsp baking powder
1 tsp salt
2/3 cup cut-up candied fruit

1/3 cup margarine or
   butter, softened
1 cup milk
1 egg

Heat oven to 350°. Prepare Streusel and set aside. Combine all of dry ingredients above in mixing bowl. Cut in softened margarine; then add milk and egg and blend on low speed for 30 seconds. Beat at medium speed for 2 minutes, scraping bowl occasionally. Stir in candied fruit and spread batter in greased 13 x 9 x 2 baking pan. Sprinkle with Streusel. Bake for 35 to 40 minutes or when wooden toothpick inserted in center comes out clean. Yields 12 servings.

STREUSEL

½ cup chopped nuts
⅓ cup packed brown sugar
¼ cup all-purpose flour

½ tsp ground cinnamon
3 tbsp firm margarine
or butter

Mix all ingredients above until crumbly.

Mincemeat Coffee Ring

2 cups all-purpose flour
2 tbsp sugar
3 tsp baking powder
1 tsp salt

$\frac{2}{3}$ cup milk
$\frac{1}{3}$ cup vegetable oil
1 cup prepared mincemeat
Lemon Glaze (next page)

Heat oven to 425°. Combine flour, sugar, baking powder, and salt. Stir in milk and oil until dough is scraped away from sides of bowl and mounds up into a ball. Knead lightly 10 times. On a lightly floured surface, shape into a 13 x 9 inch rectangle. Spread mincemeat over top and roll up tightly, beginning at 13-inch side. To seal, pinch edge of dough into roll. Shape into ring on lightly greased cookie sheet with sealed edge down and pinch ends together. Make cuts ⅔ of the way through ring with oiled scissors at 1-inch intervals. Turn each section on its side and bake for 20 to 25 minutes or until golden brown. Spread with Lemon Glaze while warm. Makes 8 to 10 servings.

LEMON GLAZE

Add 1 to 2 tsp lemon juice to ½ cup powdered sugar and beat until smooth.

Pumpkin Muffins

1 cup packed brown sugar
¾ cup vegetable oil
3 eggs
1½ cups canned pumpkin puree
3½ cups flour
2 tsp baking powder
1 tsp baking soda
1 tsp cinnamon

1 tsp grated nutmeg
½ tsp ground cloves
¼ tsp salt
1 cup unsweetened
   apple juice
½ cup chopped toasted
   walnuts
½ cup raisins

Preheat oven to 375°. Line muffin tin with 18 paper baking cups. Beat brown sugar and oil in a large bowl with electric mixer until light and fluffy. Add eggs, one at a time, beating well after each addition. Add pumpkin puree and blend well. In another bowl, gently mix flour, baking powder, baking soda, cinnamon, nutmeg, cloves, and salt. Add apple juice and dry mixture alternately to pumpkin mixture, beginning and ending with dry ingredients. Mix in walnuts and raisins. Pour batter into muffin cups and bake 20 to 25 minutes or until tops are golden and bounce back when touched.

Yogurt and Blueberry Scones

3 cups flour
2 tsp baking powder
1 tsp baking soda
½ tsp salt
2 tbsp brown sugar
6 tbsp cold butter

1¼ cups plain yogurt
2 eggs
½ cup blueberries,
   fresh or frozen
¼ tsp cinnamon

Preheat oven to 400°. Grease a cookie sheet and set aside. Combine flour, baking powder, baking soda, salt, and brown sugar in a medium bowl. Stir gently until well mixed. Using largest holes of a box grater, grate cold butter into flour mixture and stir in as you grate to avoid butter sticking together. Create a well in center and add 1 egg and yogurt. Stir in blueberries dusted with cinnamon until just combined. Scoop dough onto cookie sheet using a ¼-cup measure. Beat remaining egg and brush on top of each scone. Bake 12 to 15 minutes, or until golden brown, and serve immediately.

Whole Wheat Popovers

4 eggs
2 cups milk
1½ cups all-purpose flour

½ cup whole wheat flour
1 tsp salt

Heat oven to 450°. Grease twelve 6-ounce custard cups. Slightly beat eggs. Add milk, flours, and salt, and beat just until smooth, taking care not to overbeat. Fill custard cups about ½ full and bake for 20 minutes at 450°. Reduce heat to 350° and bake for 15 to 20 minutes longer, or until golden brown. Remove from cups immediately and serve hot.

5
MAIN DISHES

We hear the Christmas Angels
The great glad tidings tell;
O come to us, abide with us
Our Lord Emmanuel!

Roast Turkey with Chicken Sausage Stuffing

4 tbsp vegetable oil
1 pound chicken or
    turkey sausage,
    removed from casing
1 large onion, chopped
2 celery ribs, chopped
3 cups cubed stale
    pumpernickel bread

2 large eggs
1 turkey (10–12 pound)
    thawed if frozen
1 tsp sage
1 tsp paprika
$\frac{1}{2}$ tsp salt
$\frac{1}{4}$ tsp pepper
2 cups chicken broth

Heat 2 tbsp oil in a large skillet over medium heat.
Add sausage and cook 5 to 7 minutes or until lightly browned. Turn into large bowl and set aside. Heat remaining 2 tbsp oil in same frying pan and add onion and celery, cooking 3 to 5 minutes or until tender. Add to bowl with sausage and cool. Mix eggs and bread crumbs well. Preheat oven to 350°. Remove neck and giblets from turkey and rinse turkey inside and out. Pat dry and season turkey with sage, paprika, salt, and pepper. Stuff loosely with filling. Place turkey in large roasting pan with breast side up. Pour chicken broth around turkey and roast for 3½ to 4 hours, or until roast is tender and juices run clear when thigh is pricked with a fork. Baste every 30 minutes.

Roast Beef with Yorkshire Pudding

Place 4 to 6 pound boneless rib roast on rack in shallow roasting pan with fat side up. Sprinkle with salt and pepper and insert meat thermometer in thickest part of beef, avoiding fat. Roast in 325° oven uncovered for about $1\frac{3}{4}$ hours to desired degree of doneness: 130–135° for rare, and 150–155° for medium. Shortly before beef is done, prepare Yorkshire Pudding Batter (next page). Remove beef from oven and transfer to platter; cover with aluminum foil. Heat a 9 x 9 x 2-inch baking pan in oven at 425°. Reserve $\frac{1}{4}$ cup meat drippings, adding vegetable oil if necessary, and pour into heated pan. Add pudding batter and bake 25 minutes or until puffed and golden brown. Cut into squares and serve with sliced roast beef. Also good with Roast Beef Gravy (see "Side Dishes").

YORKSHIRE PUDDING BATTER

1 cup all-purpose flour	2 eggs
1 cup milk	$\frac{1}{2}$ tsp salt

Beat all ingredients until smooth.

Lasagna

1 pound Italian sausage
1 clove garlic, minced
1 tbsp whole basil
1½ tsp salt
1 can (1-pound) tomatoes
2 cans (6-ounces) tomato paste
10 ounces lasagna noodles
2 eggs

3 cups fresh Ricotta or
  cream-style cottage cheese
½ cup grated Parmesan or
  Romano cheese
2 tbsp parsley flakes
1 tsp salt
½ tsp pepper
1 pound mozzarella cheese,
  sliced very thin

Brown sausage slowly and spoon off excess fat. Add next 5 ingredients plus 1 cup of water and simmer, covered, for 15 minutes; stir frequently. Cook noodles in boiling salted water till tender. Beat eggs and add remaining ingredients except mozzarella. Layer half the lasagna noodles in 13 x 9 x 2 inch baking dish; spread with half of Ricotta filing; then half of mozzarella cheese and half of meat sauce. Repeat. Bake at 375° for 30 minutes. Serves 8 to 10.

Honey Roast Ham

4½ pound cured ham,
   leg or shoulder roast
1 onion
cloves
2 bay leaves

a few black peppercorns
twist of orange peel
small piece of fresh ginger
½ cinnamon stick
few stalks of parsley

GLAZE

Cloves
6 tbsp clear honey

2 tbsp whole grain
   mustard

Calculate cooking time for ham, figuring 20 minutes per pound, adding an extra 20 minutes. In order to draw off salt used in curing process, place ham in a large pan and cover with cold water. Bring to a boil and remove from heat. Pour off water and replace with cold water, adding onion, cloves, and other flavoring ingredients. Bring to a boil slowly, cover and simmer for calculated time, subtracting 15 minutes. Remove ham from pan and cool slightly. Heat oven to 350°. Score fat of ham in diamond pattern with sharp knife and press cloves into fat at intervals. Combine honey and mustard and spread over skin. Wrap ham in foil, leaving glazed area uncovered. Bake in roasting pan for 15 minutes. Serve hot or cold. Serves 8–10.

Herbed Salmon Steaks

2 tbsp margarine or butter
2 tbsp lemon juice
4 salmon steaks, 3/4 inch thick
1 tsp onion salt
1/4 tsp pepper

1/2 tsp dried marjoram or
   thyme leaves
paprika
lemon wedges
parsley

Place margarine and lemon juice in a 12 x 7 1/2 x 2 inch baking dish and heat in a 400° oven. Coat both sides of fish with lemon butter and place in baking dish. Sprinkle with seasonings and bake uncovered about 25 minutes, or until fish flakes easily with fork. Sprinkle with paprika and serve with lemon wedges and parsley. Serves 4.

Savory Pork Roast

4 pound pork boneless
   top loin roast
1 clove garlic, cut into halves

1 tsp dried sage leaves
1 tsp dried marjoram leaves
1 tsp salt

Using cut sides of garlic, rub pork roast. After mixing remaining ingredients, sprinkle on roast and place fat side up in shallow roasting pan. Insert meat thermometer in thickest part of pork and roast uncovered in a 325° oven for 2 to 2½ hours, or until meat thermometer registers 170°. Garnish with frosted grapes (dipped in water and rolled in sugar) if desired.

Roast Goose with Browned Potatoes

1 goose (9 to 11 pounds)
4 to 6 large potatoes, pared
   and cut into halves

salt and pepper
paprika

Remove excess fat from goose. Lightly rub salt into cavity of goose. With skewer, fasten neck skin to back. Fold wings across back with tips touching and tie drumsticks to tail. Pierce skin liberally with fork. Place goose in shallow roasting pan breast side up and roast uncovered in a 350° oven for 3 to 3½ hours, removing excess fat from pan occasionally. One hour and 15 minutes before goose is done, place potatoes around goose in roasting pan. Brush potatoes with goose drippings and sprinkle with salt, pepper, and paprika. Place a tent of aluminum foil loosely over goose to prevent excessive browning if necessary. After baking, cover and let stand 15 minutes for easier carving. Serve with Roast Goose Gravy and Raisin and Pecan Stuffing (see "Side Dishes").

Herbed Cornish Hens

3 frozen Rock Cornish hens
   (about 1 pound each), thawed
salt and pepper
1/4 cup margarine or butter, melted

1/2 tsp dried marjoram leaves
1/2 tsp dried thyme leaves
1/4 tsp paprika

Rub salt and pepper into cavities of hens. Combine margarine, marjoram, thyme, and paprika; brush portion of mixture on hens that have been placed in shallow baking pan, breast side up. Roast uncovered in 350° oven, brushing with remaining margarine mixture 5 or 6 times until done (about 1 hour). Cut each hen into halves with scissors, cutting along backbone from tail to neck and down center of breast. Garnish with watercress.

6

SIDE DISHES

The cooks shall be busied, by day and by night,
In roasting and boiling, for taste and delight.
Although the cold weather doth hunger provoke,
'Tis a comfort to see how the chimneys do smoke. . .

ANONYMOUS

scalloped oysters

2 cups oyster crackers
1 pint oysters
½ cup heavy cream
¼ tsp salt

⅛ tsp freshly
  ground pepper
1 tbsp chopped parley
2 tbsp butter

Preheat oven to 425°. Grease a 9 x 13 baking dish, placing half of crackers on bottom layer. Top with oysters. Drizzle ¼ cup cream over oysters and season with half of salt and pepper. Sprinkle with chopped parsley and spread remaining crackers, cream, salt, and pepper over top. Dot with butter and bake 20 to 25 minutes or until bubbly and lightly browned.

Duchess Potatoes

instant mashed potatoes   1 egg
paprika

Prepare instant mashed potatoes to serve four according to package directions, but decrease milk to 2 tablespoons. In a small bowl, beat 1 egg slightly; add hot potatoes and beat at medium speed until fluffy. Drop by teaspoonfuls onto greased cookie sheet and sprinkle with paprika. Bake in 400° oven for about 15 minutes or until golden brown.

Holiday salad

2 cups boiling water
1 package (6 ounces)
    lime-flavored gelatin
1 can (20 ounces) crushed
    pineapple, drained
    (reserve syrup)
1 package (8 ounces)
    cream cheese, softened

¾ cup whipping cream
½ cup finely chopped
    celery
2 tbsp mayonnaise or
    salad dressing
salad greens

Place gelatin in a 1½-quart bowl and pour boiling water over top. Stir until dissolved. Add enough water to reserved pineapple syrup to measure 1 cup and stir into gelatin. Pour ½ cup gelatin into a 7-cup mold or baking pan, 9 x 9 x 2 inches. Chill until firm. Blend remaining gelatin into cream cheese until smooth. Refrigerate for 1 to 1½ hours or until slightly thickened. Beat until smooth. In another chilled bowl, beat whipping cream until stiff. Fold mayonnaise, celery, whipped cream, and pineapple into gelatin mixture and pour out over gelatin in mold. Chill 2 hours or until firm. Remove salad from mold onto salad greens.

Ham and Broccoli Scallop

1 package (5.5 ounces) au gratin potato mix
1½ to 2 cups cubed fully cooked smoked ham
1 package (10 ounces) frozen chopped broccoli,
   partially thawed and broken apart

Prepare potatoes according to package directions, but omit margarine and use casserole. Stir in ham and broccoli. Cook uncovered 45 to 50 minutes.

oyster stew

3 tbsp unsalted butter
2 pints fresh oysters
½ tsp salt
¼ tsp ground mace

¼ tsp white pepper
pinch cayenne
2 cups milk
2 cups light cream

Melt butter in a large heavy saucepan over medium-low heat. Add oysters and seasonings. Cook about 5 minutes, or until oysters plump up and edges just begin to curl. In another saucepan, cook milk and cream over medium heat being careful not to boil or scorch. Add hot milk mixture to cooked oysters, mixing well, and serve at once in heated bowls. Serves 6 to 8.

White and Wild Rice Medley

½ cup slivered almonds
¼ cup uncooked wild rice
1 jar (2½ ounces) sliced
  mushrooms, drained
2 tbsp chopped green onions

¼ cup margarine or butter
1 tbsp instant chicken bouillon
2½ cups boiling water
¾ cup uncooked regular rice

Melt margarine in skillet and add almonds, wild rice, mushrooms, and green onion. Cook and stir for 10 to 15 minutes until almonds are golden brown. Pour into ungreased 1½-quart casserole. Stir in instant bouillon and water. Cover and cook in 350° oven for 30 minutes. Mix in regular rice. Cover and cook about 30 minutes longer until liquid is absorbed. Serves 6.

Fresh Cranberry Salad

2 cups water
¾ cup sugar
3 cups (12 ounces) cranberries
1 package (6 ounces)
   orange-flavored gelatin

1 can (8¼ ounces) crushed
   pineapple
½ cup chopped celery or
   walnuts
salad greens

Place water and sugar in a 2-quart saucepan and bring to a boil; boil 1 minute. Add cranberries and return to a boil for 5 minutes. Add gelatin and stir until dissolved. Stir in celery and pineapple (including liquid). Pour into a 6-cup mold and chill at least 6 hours until firm. Unmold on salad greens. May be garnished with pineapple chunks and sour cream.

Roast Goose Gravy

giblets from goose, washed
1 onion, skinned and quartered
4 cloves
1/2 lemon, roughly cut
slice of orange peel
1 stalk celery, sliced

1 carrot, sliced
4 2/3 cups water
1 tbsp all-purpose flour
salt and freshly
    ground black pepper

Place first 7 ingredients in a pan and cover with water. Bring to a boil and skim off foam that rises to surface. Cover and simmer for 1 hour. With juices reserved from baked goose, stir in flour over low heat. Add stock from first mixture and stir until gravy is smooth and thick.

Roast and Pecan Stuffing for Goose

1 large onion, chopped
6 stalks celery, finely chopped
3 tbsp water
1½ cups fresh white
    bread crumbs
⅔ cup seedless raisins
1 cup pecans, chopped

grated rind and juice of
    1 orange
2 eggs, beaten
grated nutmeg
salt and freshly ground
black pepper

Simmer onion and celery in small pan with water for about 5 minutes until tender. Place vegetables in a bowl and stir in bread crumbs, raisins, nuts, orange rind, juice, and eggs. Season to taste with nutmeg, salt, and pepper. Allow to cool, then pack in goose.

Roast Beef Gravy

1 tbsp all-purpose flour

1½ cups meat or
vegetable stock

Pour off fat from roasting pan and add flour to remaining drippings. Stir over medium heat gradually pouring in stock water. Bring to a boil and season with salt and pepper.

Apple Sauce

2 large cooking apples, peeled,
   cored and chopped
2 tbsp apple juice
1 tbsp butter

1 tbsp light brown sugar
1 star anise seedpod
salt and freshly ground
   black pepper

Place all ingredients except salt and pepper in pan and cook over medium heat, uncovered for 15 minutes, stirring occasionally until fruit is soft. Remove the star anise and puree fruit in a food processor. Season with salt and pepper.

7

DESSERTS

Oh, a wonderful pudding! Bob Cratchit said, and calmly too,
that he regarded it as the greatest success achieved by
Mrs. Cratchit since their marriage. . . .
Then Bob proposed:
"A Merry Christmas to us all my dears. God bless us!"
"God bless us every one!" said Tiny Tim, the last of all.
CHARLES DICKENS,
A Christmas Carol

Red currant and Black currant Kissel

1 pound red currants
1 pound black currants
²/₃ cup water

5 tbsp clear honey
2 tbsp cornstarch
berries and leaves to garnish

Place fruit in a large pan with water and honey over low heat and bring just to a boil, stirring occasionally. Put cornstarch into a small bowl and stir in 3 tbsp of juice from fruit. Pour mixture into the pan and stir over low heat until thick and glossy. Cool and pour into a serving dish. Garnish with leaves and berries if desired. Serves 8.

chocolate Nesselrode cake

One of the traditional flavors of Christmastime, nesselrode was originally a pudding created by the chef to a nineteenth century Russian count of the same name.

2 cups all-purpose flour
2 cups sugar
1 tsp baking soda
1 tsp salt
½ tsp baking powder
¾ cup water
¾ cup buttermilk

½ cup shortening
2 eggs
1 tsp vanilla
4 ounces melted unsweetened
    chocolate (cool)
Nesselrode Filling (page 106)
Cocoa Fluff (page 106)

Heat oven to 350°. Grease and flour three 8-inch round cake pans. Mix all ingredients except Nesselrode Filling and Cocoa Fluff in large mixing bowl on low speed approximately 30 seconds, scraping bowl constantly. Beat three more minutes on high speed, scraping occasionally. Pour into cake pans and bake for 30 to 35 minutes until wooden pick inserted in center comes out clean. Cool and fill layers and frost top of cake with Nesselrode Filling. Use Cocoa Fluff to frost sides. Refrigerate.

Nesselrode Filling

Place 1 cup whipping cream and ¼ cup powdered sugar in chilled bowl and beat until stiff. Fold in ¼ cup Nesselrode (¼ cup finely cut-up candied fruit stirred with 1 tsp rum flavoring)

COCOA FLUFF

Beat 1 cup whipping cream, ¼ cup powdered sugar, and 2 tbsp cocoa in chilled bowl until stiff.

Old-Fashioned Plum Pudding

3 eggs
½ pound raisins
½ pound currants
2 ounces citron (chopped)
1 pound flour (4 cups)
2 tsp nutmeg

½ tsp cinnamon
½ pound sugar
½ pound suet
   chopped fine
milk (enough for
   stiff batter)

Separate yolks from whites of eggs. Sprinkle fruit and citron with flour. Combine dry ingredients. Add egg yolks and mix thoroughly, then add enough milk to make a stiff batter. Fold in beaten egg whites last. Turn into thickly floured square of unbleached cotton cloth, tie securely, leaving some space for pudding to swell, and plunge into boiling water. Boil gently five hours. Remove pudding and allow to cool. If stored in a cool, dry, airy place, puddings may keep well for 1 year!

Epiphany Jam Tart

4 to 4½ cups flour
½ tsp salt
⅔ cup sugar
½ tsp cinnamon
1½ cups (¾ pound) unsalted
    butter, slightly softened

2 eggs
4 hard-boiled egg yolks,
    sieved
2 to 4 tbsp milk
grated rind of 1 lemon

different-colored thick jams: strawberry, raspberry, gooseberry,
    orange marmalade, pineapple, quince, prune, etc.
1 egg yolk beaten with 1 tbsp milk

Sift together dry ingredients into a wide bowl and cut butter into mixture, using a pastry blender, until mixture resembles fine meal. Stir together eggs, yolks, milk, and lemon rind, and pour into a well in center of flour mixture. Using a fork, work ingredients together until dough sticks together in a ball. Knead dough until smooth and wrap in waxed paper; chill for 30 minutes. Divide dough into two equal parts. Roll out first between waxed paper to 1/4-inch thickness and place in bottom of pie plate. Roll out other half in circle of the same size. From this, cut a 1-inch ring that will fit around edge of pie plate. Cut remaining dough into strips to form star pattern across pie plate and secure with already-cut ring of pastry around pie plate. Spoon as many different-colored jams as possible into spaces between lattice strips; brush strips with egg yolk glaze and bake in oven preheated to 350° for 30 to 45 minutes. Makes a 9-inch tart.

Cream Puffs

1 cup water
½ cup margarine or butter
1 cup all-purpose flour

4 eggs
Eggnog Fluff Filling
(next page)

Heat oven to 400°. Bring water and margarine to a rolling boil in 1-quart saucepan. Add flour and stir vigorously over low heat about 1 minute or until mixture forms a ball. Remove from heat. Add eggs and beat until smooth. Drop ¼-cup measures of dough onto ungreased cookie sheet three inches apart. Bake 35 to 40 minutes, until puffed and golden. Cool. Slice off tops of puffs and remove any filaments of soft dough. Fill puffs with eggnog fluff filling and replace tops. Before serving, sprinkle with powdered sugar. Makes 10 to 12 cream puffs.

Eggnog Fluff Filling

1 package (3¾ ounces)
   vanilla instant pudding
1 cup milk
1 tsp rum flavoring

1 tsp ground nutmeg
¼ tsp ground ginger
2 cups whipping cream
powdered sugar

In large mixer bowl, blend on low speed pudding, milk, rum flavoring, nutmeg, and ginger. Add whipping cream and beat on high speed 1 to 2 minutes, until soft peaks form.

chocolate pecan cake

1½ cups semisweet
  chocolate chips
⅔ cup butter cut into pieces
4 eggs
⅓ cup superfine sugar

1 tsp vanilla extract
1 cup pecans, ground
28 pecan halves
leaves and berries
  for garnish

FROSTING

¾ cup semisweet chocolate chips
⅔ cup butter, cut into pieces

2 tbsp clear honey

Preheat oven to 350°. Line an 8-inch cake pan with non-stick baking paper. Melt chocolate and butter in a small pan over low heat, stirring constantly. Remove from heat. In mixing bowl beat eggs, sugar, and vanilla until light. Pour chocolate mixture and pecans into second mixture and blend well. Pour into prepared cake pan and bake for 25–30 minutes until center springs back when touched. Cool on a wire rack. For frosting, melt chocolate, butter, and honey over low heat. Remove from heat and dip pecan halves to coat half-way. Spread on non-stick baking paper to dry. Turn cake upside down on wire rack and peel off baking paper. Spread frosting over cake and arrange pecans in a pattern around the edge and in the center. When frosting is set, transfer to a serving plate and garnish with leaves and berries. Serves 8.

Cranberry-Angel Trifle

1 cup whipping cream
1 package (3¾ ounces) instant
  vanilla pudding
1 tsp almond extract
½ white angel food cake, torn into
  1-inch pieces (8 to 10 cups)

1 jar (14 ounces)
  cranberry-orange relish
Toasted Slivered Almonds
  (next page)

Beat whipped cream in chilled bowl until stiff. Prepare pudding according to package directions. Fold whipped cream and almond extract into pudding. Layer alternately cake pieces, then cranberry-orange relish, and finally pudding mixture in a 3-quart serving bowl. Sprinkle with toasted almonds and chill at least 5 hours. Makes 12 to 15 servings.

TOASTED SLIVERED ALMONDS
Bake 2 to 3 tbsp of slivered almonds in a shallow baking pan at 350° for about 5 minutes, until light brown.

Cheese Danish

2 tubes of crescent rolls
2 packages (8-ounce) cream cheese,
   softened
½ cup white sugar

½ cup brown sugar
1 tsp vanilla
1 tsp cinnamon
1 stick butter or margarine

Put 1 package of rolls on the bottom of a 9 x 13 ungreased pan. Pat seams closed. Beat cream cheese, vanilla, and white sugar until smooth. Place second package of crescent rolls on top. Melt butter with cinnamon and pour over top. Sprinkle with brown sugar and bake in 350° oven for 30–35 minutes.

Old~Fashioned Mince Pie

pastry for 9-inch, two-crust pie
1 jar (28 ounces) prepared
   mincemeat

1½ cups diced, pared,
   tart apples

Heat oven to 425°. Combine prepared mincemeat and tart apples; pour into pastry-lined pie plate. Cover with top crust; slit, seal, and flute. Place strip of aluminum foil around pie edge to prevent excessive browning and remove during last 15 minutes of baking. Bake 40 to 45 minutes, until golden brown.

8

COOKIES

May joy come from God above
To all those who Christmas love.

THIRTEENTH-CENTURY CAROL

Chocolate-Almond Teacakes

¾ cup margarine or butter,
   softened
⅓ cup powdered sugar
1 cup all-purpose flour

½ cup instant cocoa mix
½ cup toasted diced almonds
powdered sugar

Combine margarine and ⅓ cup powdered sugar. Stir in flour, cocoa mix, and almonds. (Refrigerate until firm if dough is too soft to shape.) Heat oven to 325°. Shape dough into 1-inch balls and place on an ungreased cookie sheet. Bake about 20 minutes, or until set. Dip tops into powdered sugar while still warm. Let cool and dip again. Yields 4 dozen cookies.

Turtle Cookies

½ cup packed brown sugar
½ cup margarine or butter,
    softened
2 tbsp water
1 tsp vanilla
1½ cups all-purpose flour

⅛ tsp salt
pecan halves
8 caramels, each cut
    into fourths
Chocolate Glaze
    (next page)

Combine brown sugar, margarine, water and vanilla. Stir in flour and salt until dough holds together. (Add 1 to 2 tsp of water if dough is dry.) Heat oven to 350°. Place 3 to 5 pecan halves in a group for each cookie on an ungreased cookie sheet. Shape dough by teaspoonfuls around caramel pieces; press firmly onto the center of each group of nuts. Bake until set, but do not brown, for 12 to 15 minutes. Cool; then dip tops of cookies into Chocolate Glaze. Yields 2½ dozen cookies.

CHOCOLATE GLAZE

In a separate bowl, beat 1 cup of confectioner's sugar, 1 tbsp water, 1 ounce melted unsweetened chocolate (cool), and 1 tsp vanilla until smooth. Stir in water, 1 tsp at a time, until frosting reaches desired consistency.

Delicate Lemon Squares

CRUST:

1 cup all-purpose flour   ½ cup butter
¼ cup powdered sugar

FILLING:

2 eggs   2 tbsp all-purpose flour
¾ cup granulated sugar   ½ tsp baking powder
3 tbsp fresh lemon juice   powdered sugar

Mix flour and powdered sugar and cut in butter until mixture clings together. Press into an ungreased 8 x 8 x 2 baking pan; bake at 350° for 10–12 minutes. In another mixing bowl beat eggs; add granulated sugar and lemon juice, and beat until thick and smooth, about 8–10 minutes. Stir together flour and baking powder, and add to egg mixture, blending until all ingredients are moistened. Pour egg mixture gently over baked crust. Bake at 350° for 20–25 minutes. Cool slightly and sift powdered sugar over top. When cool, cut cookies into 1½ inch squares. Yields 3 dozen bars.

Magic Window Cookies

1 cup sugar
³/₄ cup shortening
   (part margarine or butter,
   softened)
2 eggs

1 tsp vanilla or ¹/₂ tsp
   lemon extract
2¹/₂ cups all-purpose flour
1 tsp baking powder
1 tsp salt

about 5 rolls (about .79 ounce each) ring-shaped hard candy

Combine sugar, shortening, eggs, and vanilla. Add flour, baking powder, and salt. Cover and refrigerate at least 1 hour. On a lightly floured cloth-covered board, roll dough ⅛ inch thick. Cut into desired shapes with cookie cutters. Place cookies on a cookie sheet that has been covered with aluminum foil. Using smaller cutters, cut out centers of cookies and place whole or partially crushed candy in remaining center. (Since candy melts easily, there is no need to crush it finely.) If cookies will be hung from Christmas tree to enjoy "stained-glass" effect, make a hole ¼ inch from top with the end of a plastic straw. Heat oven to 375°. Bake 7 to 9 minutes, or until cookies are very light brown and candy is melted. If candy has not filled out cutout center, spread immediately with a metal spatula. Cool completely on cookie sheet. Yields 6 dozen 3-inch cookies.

Chocolate-Caramel Crunch Bars

1 package (14 ounces) caramels
   (about 48)
⅓ cup water
2 cups all-purpose flour
2 cups quick-cooking oats
1 cup packed brown sugar

1 cup margarine or butter,
   melted
½ tsp baking soda
¼ tsp salt
1 package (6 ounces)
   semisweet chocolate chips

Pre-heat oven to 350°. In a saucepan heat caramels and water over low heat, stirring frequently until melted and mixture is smooth. Combine flour, oats, brown sugar, margarine, baking soda, and salt. Set aside 1 cup of mixture for topping. Press remaining mixture in ungreased 13 x 9 x 2 inch baking pan. Bake for 10 minutes. Sprinkle chocolate chips over baked layer; drizzle with caramel mixture. Sprinkle reserved crumbly mixture over all and bake about 15 minutes or until light brown. Cool and cut into 2 x 1 inch bars. Yields 4 dozen bars.

Anise Drops

4 eggs
1¼ cups sugar
3 cups sifted flour

1¼ tbsp lightly crushed
anise seeds

Beat eggs with sugar until very thick and almost white. Add flour gradually and blend well after each addition. Stir in anise seeds. Warm cookie sheet in oven, lightly butter and then chill until completely cold. Drop dough onto cookie sheet, leaving 1 inch between cookies. Allow to dry uncovered at room temperature, overnight. Bake in preheated 300° oven for about 20 minutes, or until pale golden. Yields 7 dozen cookies.

Peanut Butter Thumbprints

1 stick unsalted butter, softened
½ cup peanut butter
1¼ cups sugar
1 egg

2 tbsps.milk
2 cups flour
⅔ cup raspberry jam

Using an electric mixer, beat together butter and peanut butter. Add sugar and beat until fluffy; then beat in egg and milk. Add flour, stirring with a spoon until a thick dough is formed. Place in a small, covered bowl and refrigerate at least 2 hours or until well chilled. Preheat oven to 350°. Roll dough into 1-inch balls and place 2 inches apart on a buttered cookie sheet. Gently flatten balls with the palm of your hand and make a small indentation in each with thumbtip. Fill each indentation with ½ tsp of jam. Bake for 13 to 15 minutes, or until edges are lightly browned.

Pecan Florentines

¾ cup pecan halves, pulverized* ¼ cup butter or margarine
½ cup all-purpose flour 2 tbsp milk
⅓ cup packed brown sugar ⅓ cup semisweet
¼ cup light corn syrup chocolate chips

*Place pecans in food processor or blender to pulverize, until thoroughly ground with a dry, not pasty texture.

Preheat oven to 350°. Line cookie sheets with aluminum foil and lightly grease. Mix pecans and flour together in small bowl and set aside. Stir together sugar, syrup, butter, and milk in medium saucepan. Stir over medium heat until mixture comes to a boil. Remove from heat and stir in flour mixture. Using a teaspoon, drop batter onto prepared cookie sheets about 3 inches apart. Bake 10 to 12 minutes or until lacy and golden brown. Cool completely on foil. (Cookies will harden as they cool.) Pour chocolate chips into a small, heavy-duty plastic bag and place bag in a bowl of hot water to melt chips. Knead bag to be sure all are melted, pat dry, and after snipping small corner of bag, drizzle melted chocolate over cookies to decorate. When cool, peel foil off cookies and store between layers of waxed paper in an airtight container. Yields 3 dozen cookies.

Mint Truffle Cookies

1¼ cups sugar
1 cup butter or margarine,
    softened
2 eggs
1 tsp vanilla
2½ cups all-purpose flour

¼ cup unsweetened cocoa
1 tsp baking powder
¼ tsp salt
1 package chocolate sandwich
    mints, coarsely chopped

GLAZE:

8 ounces white candy coating
1 tsp vegetable shortening

1 or 2 drops green
    food coloring

Combine sugar, butter, eggs, and vanilla in a large mixing bowl. Beat at medium speed until light and fluffy. Add four, cocoa, baking powder, and salt, and beat at low speed until a soft dough is formed. Stir in mints, cover mixture, and refrigerate for 2 to 3 hours or until firm. Heat oven to 375°. Place shaped 1-inch balls on lightly greased cookie sheet about 2 inches apart. Bake for 8 to 10 minutes and cool completely. Combine candy coating and shortening in a small saucepan and melt over low heat, stirring constantly. Stir in food coloring and drizzle over cookies, making stripes. Yields 4 dozen cookies.

Viennese Kiss Cookies

1½ cups all-purpose flour
¾ cup butter or margarine,
    chilled and cut into
    1-inch pieces

¼ cup sugar
3 tbsp sour cream
1 tsp vanilla
24 chocolate kisses

Heat oven to 350°. Grease two 12-cup miniature muffin pans and set aside. In a large mixing bowl, combine flour, butter, and sugar, and beat at medium speed until mixture resembles coarse crumbs. Add sour cream and vanilla, and beat at low speed until a soft dough forms. Shape dough into 1-inch balls. Place 1 ball in each muffin cup and bake for 20 to 25 minutes, or until edges are golden brown. Immediately press kiss into center of each cookie. Cool for 1 minute before removing from pans. Yields 2 dozen cookies.

French Christmas Cookies

½ cup butter or other shortening (softened)
¾ cup sugar
½ cup honey

2 egg yolks
¼ cup milk
1 tsp vanilla
3 cups sifted cake flour

Cream butter and sugar together until light. Add honey and egg yolks, beating well after each addition. Add milk and vanilla. Add flour in small amounts until well blended. Chill dough for 2 hours. Roll ⅛ inch thick on lightly floured board. Cut into desired shapes and bake on ungreased cookie sheets for 10 minutes at 375°. Cool and frost. Yields 3 dozen cookies.

orange-spiced shortbread

2¼ cups all-purpose flour
⅔ cup sugar
1 tsp grated orange peel
¼ to ½ tsp ground nutmeg

pinch of salt
1¼ cups butter, chilled,
   cut into small pieces

Heat oven to 325°. Lightly grease two 8-inch-square baking pans and set aside. Combine flour, sugar, peel, nutmeg, and salt in a large mixing bowl. Using pastry blender, cut in butter until mixture has the texture of coarse crumbs. Shape dough into a ball and divide in half, pressing halves evenly into prepared pans. Prick dough with a fork at 1-inch intervals. Bake for 30 to 35 minutes, or until light golden brown. Cut immediately into 2-inch squares; then cut each square diagonally to form triangles. Cool completely in pans before storing. Yields 5⅓ dozen cookies.

Chocolate-Dipped Hazelnut Biscotti

1 cup slivered almonds
1½ cups sugar
½ cup unsalted butter, softened
2 tbsp hazelnut extract or
    flavoring
3 eggs

3¾ cups all-purpose flour
2 tsp baking powder
pinch of salt
1 cup milk chocolate chips
2 tsp vegetable shortening
½ cup finely chopped
    hazelnuts

Heat oven to 350°. Lightly grease cookie sheets and set aside. Place almonds in an 8-inch square baking pan. Bake for 10–12 minutes or until light golden brown, stirring occasionally. Coarsely chop almonds and set aside. Combine sugar, butter, and extract, and beat at medium speed until light and fluffy. Add eggs, one at a time, beating after each addition. Add flour, baking powder, and salt, beating at low speed until soft dough forms. Stir in almonds. Divide dough into quarters and shape each quarter into a 2-inch-diameter log on a lightly floured surface. Place logs 2 inches apart on cookie sheet and bake for 30–35 minutes, or until golden brown. *Immediately* cut logs diagonally into ¾-inch slices. Place slices 1 inch apart on cookie sheets and bake for an additional 10–15 minutes, or until dry and golden brown. Cool completely.

In small saucepan, melt chocolate chips and shortening over low heat, stirring constantly. Remove from heat. Dip one end of each cookie diagonally into melted chocolate and sprinkle hazelnuts evenly over dipped ends. Let dry completely before storing.

Lemon Cheesecake Bars

1³⁄₄ cups crushed vanilla wafers   2 tbsp sugar
¹⁄₂ cup butter or margarine, melted

FILLING:

1 package (8 ounces)   1¹⁄₂ tsp grated lemon peel
   cream cheese, softened   1 tsp vanilla
¹⁄₃ cup sugar   ¹⁄₄ cup seedless raspberry
¹⁄₂ cup sour cream   preserves, melted
1 egg

Heat oven to 350°. Combine wafers, butter, and 2 tbsp sugar in a small mixing bowl. Press into ungreased 8-inch square baking pan and set aside. In another mixing bowl, mix cream cheese and ⅓ cup sugar. Beat at medium speed until smooth. Add remaining filling ingredients and beat until well blended. Spread filling evenly over first layer. Bake for 50 to 55 minutes, or until light golden brown. Cool and drizzle preserves over bars. Store in refrigerator. Yields 16 bars.

No-Bake
Peanut Butter Bars

2 cups graham cracker crumbs
1½ cups powdered sugar
1 cup chunky peanut butter
½ cup butter or margarine,
   melted

½ cup chopped salted
   peanuts
1½ cups milk
   chocolate chips

Lightly grease an 11 x 7 inch baking pan and set aside. Mix all ingredients except chocolate chips in a large mixing bowl. Press mixture into prepared pan. In a small saucepan, melt chips over low heat, stirring constantly. Spread chocolate evenly over bars. Chill until set and cut.

9
CANDIES

The children were nestled all snug in their beds,
While visions of sugar-plums danced through their heads. . . .

Clement C. Moore

coconut Macaroons

2½ cups granulated sugar
2⅓ cups (8 ounces) shredded, fresh unsweetened coconut
1 cup egg whites (whites of about 6 extra-large eggs)
1 tsp vanilla extract
⅓ cup plus 2 tbsp all-purpose flour
baker's parchment paper

Preheat oven to 350°. Butter a cookie sheet and cover with parchment paper. Mix sugar, coconut, and egg whites in the top of a double boiler and stir over boiling water until mixture reaches 170° on a candy thermometer. Remove from heat, and stir in vanilla and flour. Using a pastry bag with no nozzle, pipe macaroons about 1½ inches in diameter onto parchment paper. If you have no pastry bag, two teaspoons may be used. Bake for 15 minutes or until macaroons begin to turn pale gold. Remove from parchment and cool on a rack. Macaroons will keep for several weeks in an airtight container kept in a cool place.

Toffee

1 cup chopped pecans
¾ cup packed brown sugar

½ cup margarine or butter
½ cup semisweet
    chocolate chips

Butter a 9 x 9 x 2 inch baking pan. Spread pecans in bottom of pan. Bring brown sugar and margarine to a boil, stirring constantly. Boil over medium heat, and continue to stir for 7 minutes. Remove from heat and immediately spread mixture over pecans in pan. Sprinkle chocolate chips over hot mixture and place cookie sheet over pan until chocolate chips are melted. Smooth melted chocolate over candy and cut into ½-inch squares while hot. Chill until firm. Yields 3 dozen candies.

Chocolate Truffles

6 ounces (squares) dark
   semi-sweet chocolate
3 tbsp unsalted butter
2 tbsp powdered sugar

3 egg yolks
1 tbsp rum flavoring
½ cup finely grated
   semisweet chocolate

Melt chocolate in the top of a double boiler over boiling water. Blend in butter and sugar, and stir until sugar dissolves. Remove from heat and add egg yolks, one at a time, beating well after each addition. Stir in rum flavoring. Place in a bowl covered with wax paper overnight, but do not chill. Shape into 1-inch diameter balls and roll in grated chocolate. Eat after a day or two. Yields 2 dozen.

Sugar Plums

1 (24-ounce) container
    pitted prunes
4 ounces whole blanched
    almonds

1 cup (4 ounces)
    sweetened flaked
    coconut
¼ cup sugar

Insert an almond into each prune, molding fruit around the nut to create a plum shape. Mix coconut and sugar together in a small ball and roll stuffed prunes in mixture. Store in an airtight container with wax paper between the layers, or wrap individually. Yields about 100.

Easy Chocolate Fudge

1 cup granulated sugar
¼ cup cocoa
⅓ cup milk
¼ cup margarine or butter

1 tbsp light corn syrup
1 tsp vanilla
⅓ cup chopped nuts
2 to 2¼ cups powdered sugar

Combine granulated sugar and cocoa in a 2-quart saucepan. Stir in milk, margarine, and corn syrup. Bring to a boil over medium heat, stirring frequently. Boil and stir 1 minute. Remove from heat and allow to cool without stirring until bottom of pan is lukewarm (about 45 minutes). Stir in vanilla and nuts. Mix in powdered sugar until very stiff. Press in buttered loaf pan measuring 9 x 5 x 3 inches. Chill until firm and cut into 1-inch squares. Yields 32 candies.

Peanut Brittle

1½ tsp baking soda
1 tsp water
1 tsp vanilla
1½ cups sugar
1 cup water

1 cup light corn syrup
3 tbsp margarine or butter
1 pound shelled unroasted
  peanuts

Butter 2 cookie sheets and keep warm. Mix baking soda, water, and vanilla; set aside. Combine sugar, water, and corn syrup in a 3-quart saucepan and cook over medium heat, stirring occasionally until candy thermometer reads 240°, or until small amount of syrup dropped into very cold water forms a soft ball that can be flattened when removed from the water. Add margarine and peanuts, and cook to 300°, stirring constantly, or until small amounts of mixture separate into hard, brittle threads when dropped into very cold water. Remove from heat immediately and stir in baking soda mixture. Pour half of candy mixture onto each cookie sheet and quickly spread about ¼ inch thick. Cool and break into pieces. Yields 2 pounds of candy.

Choco~Butterscotch Crisps

1 cup butterscotch chips
½ cup peanut butter
4 cups crisped rice cereal
1 cup chocolate chips

2 tbsp butter
1 tbsp water
½ cup powdered sugar

Melt butterscotch chips and peanut butter over very low heat, stirring occasionally. Add cereal and mix well. Press half of mixture in an 8 x 8 inch square pan and chill. Melt chocolate chips, butter, and water in top of a double boiler and add powdered sugar. Spread over chilled mixture and press in remainder of cereal mixture. Cut and chill.

Molasses Taffy

2 cups very dark molasses
1 cup brown sugar, firmly packed,
   or granulated sugar

1 tbsp vinegar
2 tbsp unsalted butter

Mix molasses, sugar, and vinegar in a small but heavy saucepan and stir over low heat until sugar dissolves. Cover and boil (but do not stir) until mixture reaches 245° on a candy thermometer, or forms a firm ball when dropped into cold water. Stir in butter and simmer slowly until mixture reaches 270° on candy thermometer or crackles when dropped into cold water. Pour into a buttered pan. After taffy has cooled, rub a bland oil onto your hands and take small amounts of taffy at a time, stretching to a length of about 14 inches, folding back on itself and stretching again, until all of taffy is no longer transparent but creamy and light in color and the ends hold a shape. Pull until ½ inch in diameter and cut into small squares with a pair of oiled scissors. Cool on a rack until hardened and wrap in waxed paper. Yields about 1 pound.

cranberry fudge

4 cups granulated sugar
¼ cup unsalted butter
⅔ cup milk
1 tbsp golden (corn) syrup

1 can (7 ounce) full-cream
condensed milk
¾ cup fresh cranberries

Mix sugar, butter, milk, and corn syrup in a heavy saucepan and bring slowly to a boil, stirring constantly. Add condensed milk and return to a boil for 20 minutes, while continuing to stir, until mixture reaches 250° or when a small amount dropped into very cold water sets hard. Remove from heat and stir in cranberries. Spread in well-greased jelly roll pan and cut into squares just before fudge hardens. When completely cooled, cut into pieces and store in airtight container. Yields 2 pounds of candy.

Popcorn Balls

½ cup sugar
½ cup light corn syrup
½ cup margarine or butter

½ tsp salt
few drops food color
8 cups popped corn

Simmer sugar, corn syrup, margarine, salt, and food color in a 4-quart Dutch oven over medium-high heat, stirring constantly. Add popped corn and cook about 3 minutes, stirring constantly until popcorn is well coated. Cool slightly. After dipping hands into cold water, shape mixture into 2½ inch balls. Place on waxed paper and when cooled, wrap individually in plastic wrap. Makes 8 or 9 popcorn balls.

Crispy Cereal Chocolate Drops

2 cups (12 ounces) butterscotch chips
1 cup (6 ounces) semi-sweet chocolate chips
½ cups salted peanuts
4 cups crisp cereal (almost anything will work)

Melt butterscotch chips and chocolate chips over very low heat stirring constantly until smooth. Remove from heat. Add peanuts and cereal. Stir carefully until well coated. Drop by teaspoonfuls onto waxed paper. Chill until firm. Yields 8 dozen.

Peanut Butter Bonbons

1½ cups powdered sugar
1 cup graham cracker crumbs
   (about 12 squares)
½ cup margarine or butter

½ cup peanut butter
1 package (6 ounces)
   semisweet chocolate
   chips

Combine powdered sugar and cracker crumbs. Melt margarine and peanut butter over low heat and stir into crumb mixture. Shape into 1-inch balls. Melt chocolate chips with 1 tbsp shortening and dip balls into chocolate with tongs until coated. Place on waxed paper and chill until firm. Yields 3 dozen candies.